D1274639

A Look at China

by Helen Frost

Consulting Editor: Gail Saunders-Smith, Ph.D.

Consultant: Xiaohong Shen, Ph.D.
Assistant Director, Center for East Asian Studies
Stanford University

Pebble Books

an imprint of Capstone Press
Mankato, Minnesota

J
951
FROST

1/03
$10.95

Pebble Books are published by Capstone Press
151 Good Counsel Drive, P.O. Box 669, Mankato, Minnesota 56002
http://www.capstone-press.com

1 2 3 4 5 6 07 06 05 04 03 02

Library of Congress Cataloging-in-Publication Data
Frost, Helen, 1949–
  A look at China / by Helen Frost.
  p. cm.—(Our world)
  ISBN 0-7368-0983-X
  1. China—Juvenile literature. [1. China.] I. Title. II. Series: Our world
(Pebble Books)
  DS706 .F76 2002
  951—dc21   00-012708

Summary: Simple text and photographs depict the land, animals, and people
of China.

Note to Parents and Teachers

The Our World series supports national social studies standards
related to culture. This book describes and illustrates the land,
animals, and people of China. The photographs support early
readers in understanding the text. The repetition of words and
phrases helps early readers learn new words. This book also
introduces early readers to subject-specific vocabulary words, which
are defined in the Words to Know section. Early readers may need
assistance to read some words and to use the Table of Contents,
Words to Know, Read More, Internet Sites, and Index/Word List
sections of the book.

Table of Contents

Beijing

★

China

China is a country in eastern Asia. China is the third largest country in the world. The capital of China is Beijing.

China's flag

desert

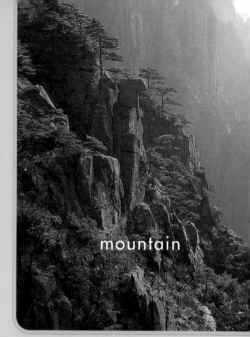

mountain

6 plateau

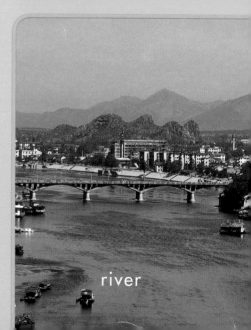

river

China has deserts,
mountains, plateaus,
and rivers. Each part of
China has different weather.

giant panda

golden monkey

Giant pandas
and golden monkeys
live in China.

10

More than one billion
people live in China.
They speak and write
Chinese. This langauge
is made up of symbols.

hello	good-bye
你好	再見
(NEE HOW)	(TSEYE JEE-en)

Many people in China use chopsticks to eat. The Chinese eat vegetables, meat, and fish. They also eat soup, rice, and noodles.

14

Chinese New Year is in the spring. Families and friends gather to celebrate. They watch parades and fireworks.

Some Chinese people work in factories to earn money. Some people are farmers. They raise rice and other crops to feed their families.

China's money is counted in Yuan.

Most people in China travel short distances by bicycle. They travel long distances by train. People also travel by boat, car, and airplane.

The Great Wall of China is more than 2,000 years old. It is about 1,500 miles (2,400 kilometers) long. Thousands of people visit the Great Wall every year.

Words to Know

Asia—the largest continent on Earth; a continent is a large land mass; there are seven continents on Earth.

capital—the city in a country where the government is based; the capital of China is Beijing.

China—a country in eastern Asia; China is the third largest country in the world by size; China has the largest population of all the countries in the world.

chopsticks—narrow sticks used to eat food; chopsticks are used mostly by people in Asian countries.

Great Wall of China—a wall that the ancient Chinese built across northern China; the wall was built to protect China's border.

language—the words and grammar that people use to talk and write to each other; the Chinese language is made up of symbols that stand for words and phrases.

plateau—an area of high, flat land

Read More

Dahl, Michael S. *China.* Countries of the World. Mankato, Minn.: Bridgestone Books, 1998.

Goh, Sui Noi, and Lim Bee Ling. *Welcome to China.* Welcome to My Country. Milwaukee: Gareth Stevens, 1999.

Mamdani, Shelby. *Cultural Journeys: Traditions from China.* Austin, Texas: Raintree Steck-Vaughn, 1999.

Ryan, Patrick. *China.* Plymouth, Minn.: Child's World, 1998.

Internet Sites

China
http://www.infoplease.com/ipa/a0107411.html

Secrets of the Great Wall
http://www.discovery.com/stories/history/greatwall/greatwall.html

Zoom School: China
http://www.enchantedlearning.com/school/China

Index/Word List

Word Count: 178
Early-Intervention Level: 17

Editorial Credits
Mari C. Schuh, editor; Kia Bielke, cover designer and illustrator; Kimberly Danger,
   photo researcher

Photo Credits
Claudia Adams/Root Resources, 20
Gary Milburn/TOM STACK & ASSOCIATES, 8 (bottom)
Inga Spence/TOM STACK & ASSOCIATES, 16
Jeff Greenberg/Photo Agora, cover, 10, 18
Kenneth W. Fink/Root Resources, 8 (top)
Mary Altier/1987, 6 (lower right)
PhotoSphere, 1
Pictor, 14
Trip/J. Batten, 6 (upper left)
Visuals Unlimited/Inga Spence, 6 (upper right); Bill Kamin, 6 (lower left); Bud
   Nielsen II, 12
Yin Chuang, 11 (inset)

The author thanks Professor Mary Steen of St. Olaf College and Suzanne Wong
Scollon, Ph.D., of Georgetown University for their assistance with this book.

24